FRASER SUTHERLAND

MANUAL FOR EMIGRANTS

.

FRASER SUTHERLAND

MANUAL FOR EMIGRANTS

TIGHTROPE BOOKS
2007

Copyright © Fraser Sutherland, 2007

ALL RIGHTS RESERVED. No part of this publication may be reproduced, stored in a retrieval system or transmitted, in any form or by any means, without prior permission of the publisher or, in the case of photocopying or other reprographic copying, a licence from Access Copyright, the Canadian Copyright Licensing Agency, www.access copyright.ca, info@accesscopyright.ca.

Tightrope Books
17 Greyton Crescent
Toronto, Ontario
Canada M6E 2G1
www.tightropebooks.com

EDITOR: Halli Villegas
COPY EDITOR: Myna Wallin
COVER DESIGN: Oleg Lipchenko
ARTWORK: Oleg Lipchenko
TYPESETTING: Carleton Wilson

Produced with the support of the Canada Council for the Arts, the Ontario Arts Council and the City of Toronto through the Toronto Arts Council.

PRINTED IN CANADA

LIBRARY AND ARCHIVES CANADA CATALOGUING IN PUBLICATION

Sutherland, Fraser
    Manual for emigrants / Fraser Sutherland.

Poems.
ISBN 978-0-9738645-9-5

    1. Title.

PS8587.U79M36 2007   C811'.54   C2007-904395-X

ACKNOWLEDGEMENTS

Some of these poems, occasionally in a different form, first appeared in the collections *Strange Ironies* (Fiddlehead Poetry Books), *In the Wake Of* and *Within the Wound* (both Northern Journey Press), *Madwomen* and *Whitefaces* (both Black Moss Press), and *Peace and War* (with Goran Simic, privately published). "Dunrobin" appeared as a privately published broadside. "Café Istanbul" and most of the poems in the section "A Manual for Emigrants" formed part of *A Ballad of Baggage*, a mixed-media performance piece staged in Toronto by Goran Simic, Aleksandar Bukvic, and Berge Arabian, directed by Antonia Miovska, and first appeared in print in the *Dhaka Independent* (Bangladesh). Other poems first appeared in *Impulse, New: American & Canadian Poetry, Sampler, Tamarack Review, Pottersfield Portfolio, Un Dozen, Relations: Family Portraits, The Idler, paperplates, Stvaranje* (Cetinje, Montenegro), and *Landmarks: An Anthology of New Atlantic Canadian Poetry of the Land*. My thanks to all the editors concerned.

Quotations in "Ode to Thomas Jefferson Sutherland" are from the *Dictionary of Canadian Biography*. "If He Goes Back" is for Goran Simic, to whom I am indebted for editorial advice.

CONTENTS

PART I: A MANUAL FOR EMIGRANTS

13 Faces
14 Mates
15 English
16 War
18 Work
19 Money
20 White
21 Art
22 Enough

PART II: THERE

25 Café Istanbul
26 Pen
27 Question asked in the Native Bar of a Lowlife Winnipeg Hotel
28 Palace Hotel do Buçaco
29 You Don't Have to Be Drunk
30 Nicaragua
31 How Are Things on Bouvet Island?
32 Loop in the River
33 Lights of Castries
35 The Arrival
36 Television
37 Good Friday
39 Serbian Headstones
40 The Man on a Horse
41 Two Serbian Girls at the Salonika Cemetary
42 Taxi Ride
43 Palestinians
44 Genocide

45 Forms of Loss
46 If He Goes Back
47 The History of Modern European Poetry
48 At the Site of an Air Disaster Memorial
50 Places by the Road

PART III: HERE

53 Welcome to Canada
54 Themes on a Variation of Snow
57 Victoria Day
58 Model
60 Chinatown
61 Toronto
62 From an Auction Catalogue
63 Kosovo
64 Hammock
65 In the Provinces
68 Whitefaces: 1982
70 History
71 New Place
72 Mr. Sachs
73 Cold House
74 Classmates
75 Heathbell School Reunion
78 Dunrobin
80 Ode to Thomas Jefferson Sutherland

PART I
A MANUAL FOR EMIGRANTS

FACES

You have a new face.

Living a life needs familiar faces, the faces of your family, of your friends.

I don't recognize your face.

Or your family. Or your friends.

Somewhere down the line you chose the wrong mask.

Turn your face to the wall; show us the blank back of the head.

Blankness is something we recognize.

MATES

You can keep your gene pool.

If we wanted something new, we'd order it.

A selection of mates is readily available on our TV screens. All we have to do is look for matches among ourselves.

We're not about to look to you as a resource we can tap, not your breeding machines chained to a bedpost, wrapped in a veil. Not your bearded men angry about Christmas trees, proud of their turbans. You'll just do what you've always done well.

No, keep to yourselves. You'll be happier that way.

We're going to write on the blank slate that is ourselves; we don't want you smudging it. Who needs to ask more questions than we already have?

Who needs you squirming into our family photographs?

ENGLISH

Speak English.

You must speak English.

The whole world will soon speak English so you might as well speak it where it's spoken first and best and most.

If you speak English we may let you stay for a while.

If you learned it before you came here, you must learn it better. But you will never learn it well enough.

Don't speak gibberish.

Speak English.

This applies everywhere in Canada except Québec.

Where you must speak French.

WAR

You have war in your luggage but they let you through airport customs anyway.

We have learned to fight our small tedious fights, learned to bore each other with our demands, learned to fall asleep to grievances. We spend half our time in court. This is called the rule of law.

You do things differently.

We don't want your warlords, your rapes and death camps, your borders erased and redrawn, your revenge and your resentments. We don't want your wars.

And when you walk along the street in tight or baggy clothes we can hear you muttering: *My neighbour poisoned my well. He set my temple on fire, it burned to the ground. The bomb went off just as we were buying bread.*

You're in the import-export business, watching, waiting to get back at him, shipping guns and plastic where they can do their worst. If you can get away with it, you would do it here.

You specialize in victims. You think you have a monopoly on misery, that you expire more painfully, that we don't know suffering.

Believe me, people die here, too. Sometimes not even in their beds.

You come here because you can't live with each other there. You should try it sometime, living with each other.

You can't.

So from time to time we have to go over and sort you out.

WORK

You don't know what work is, do you?

Those ten hours you spend waiting tables, mangling the orders we give you, your early morning circuit of neighbourhoods dropping flyers that lay waste to our forests, your stooping and reaching on assembly lines that turn out taxis whose drivers pick us up without the faintest clue where we live.

That isn't work. That's soft stuff, sissy stuff, city stuff. You can only survive in a city. You're the parasites. We're the hosts.

Real work? Go to the country.

Go down a mine, face against hard rock, the whole day in lamplit darkness.

Let your face get so red riding a tractor back and forth across a field as big as the place you came from.

Pickle your hands, swelling your knuckles in brine from which you extract fewer and fewer fish.

Bust your leg every time a giant tree falls the wrong way.

Learn what work is for a change.

MONEY

Admit it, you came for the money.

And there's money here. Our money. The money we earned freezing in the dark the centuries you were not here. The money smells of flour, floorboards, it smells of fish. It has the whiff of America.

You build land flip towel shopping plaza on falmers' fields, make-lotsa money.

You don't get money that way, we give you handouts for being who you are.

So you get money.

What do you do with the money?

You send it off to your bombsites, your barrios, your famine villages. You buy the airfare for more of you to come and take more money and send it back.

A home that isn't here.

Admit it, you came for the money.

Why else would anyone come?

WHITE

What's so wrong about white?

Where do you get off with your skin?

Didn't they tell you you'd be here for the winter. What's winter? It's white.

Step off the plane in a blizzard, do that. Learn what we put up with.

Go back. Go back to your sunbright islands, back to the hot stones of your deserts, back to your monsoons. Let it darken your skin dry or wet, darker than it's ever been. Leave our white alone.

We don't want your ink on our page.

ART

If by chance you come here to make art you are in for a surprise.

We may give you grants but no one will listen to you.

There's too much static, the din of media. If it takes you up, it will turn your art into something else, our noise.

Art needs things we cannot supply you with.

Like a thug in power who will not let you speak and, should you speak, will kill you for a word.

Like the streams of blood an artist needs to sate a vampire's appetite.

Long ago we did the killing we had to do. We lost that material.

Artists don't need grief counsellors. They need unhappy childhoods.

Art needs a civil war. Which does not happen unless you bring us one.

This is why you're not wanted.

This is why we don't have art.

Which is a good thing.

ENOUGH

We have enough prairies, mountains, lakes, and seas.

We have enough people to walk, climb, and swim in them. Enough room for them to do it. Enough room to go around for people who don't know anywhere else to be. Who don't want to be anything else than what they are.

Us.

We keep our distance. That's how we get along.

We don't want your sweat, your cooking smells, the jabber of your markets, what you call music leaking out from under your closed doors, worse your open doors. You want to huddle, you can huddle where you came from.

Don't get in the way of our distance.

PART II

THERE

The past is another country, they do things differently there.
– L. P. Hartley, *The Go-Between*

CAFÉ ISTANBUL

Seen through the window
smoking, drinking, womanless,
they are doomed men.

I don't know what they do in there
or I do: the slap of cards,
the crash of dominoes.

The street has nothing to do with them,
doubly separate.
The flag on the wall has something.

They will probably go home at some point
but they may spend
the rest of their lives here,

earnestly melancholy,
knowing each other.

PEN

The pen's in my inside pocket,
a metal reproach.
Surely people have died for lifting it
but here, where no one dies this way,
it's hardly worth the effort.
Yet the pen asks to be driven
in its shallow groove across something
that will take it, a paper napkin
with which you wipe your mouth
leaving an inky stain.
The stain is someone's blood.

QUESTION ASKED IN THE NATIVE BAR OF A LOWLIFE WINNIPEG HOTEL

"Why do you drink with people like us?"

Because I grew up where everyone was the same, and I like difference.

Because I am not guilty. I did not destroy your people, and what my forbears did belongs to history, they scratched their living, imponderable in going wrong.

Because drunk, brawling, squalling, puking, bumming beer and cigarettes from me not willing to offer more you have a greater dignity than the happy hour mate-seekers of the singles bar meat market who have their lonely dramas too I know though it would take a hefty hack to cleave through the veneer but

Because here it all breaks down, the lines, the barriers you dance if you want to, if you want to drink you do and do and do, something like freedom here, shadows taking shape the sacred that's passed you by but may return a ghost, guest, or resident.

Because however bad it gets for me, and relatively speaking it's not bad at all, you can summon something worse.

Because though we pass this way but once, you pass out many times.

Because though to people like you in this subarctic third world annex I appear a professor or a priest the colours of our skins belong to and blend within the dark we are alike though you will never know it unless, until we meet now, in this place, like this.

PALACE HOTEL DO BUÇACO

Before assassination, deposition, Empire's last
gesture wove this stony Manueline tracery,
massive like its bronze torchères, gossamer
as the wisteria drooping from its trellis.
Under candelabra, the tourists play cards.
By day a gorgeous swan's in pitted combat
with a workman digging a drain who's
heir to a revolution. The Manuel who built this
dreamt he was Ludwig of Bavaria
dreaming he was Portuguese. The royal cook
took it over after the last Bragança
fled to a villa in Twickenham.

As I sip a scotch-and-soda which
will nastily reappear on my check-out bill
I look about at the frail, stooped, stout,
the grey, the bald, and suppose that they
can afford their nights more than me.
But I don't enquire into their source of income
and hope they will not into mine
lest we find it charity, blackmail,
extortion, receiving stolen goods.

YOU DON'T HAVE TO BE DRUNK

You don't have to be drunk
to like Abba's shibboleth songs
and the line the lead sings.
She sings something about the sea.
She saw the sea, she ploughs the sea,
or is she beside the sea?
Which seems odd in landlocked Stuttgart
among melancholy men who silently sip
at their benches along the bar
in this dim place called Martinsklause
with Balkan specialties,
one of which is loneliness.
Now some other junk plays
and the pregnant gypsy-dark waitress with bruised arms,
bringing someone else into the world,
takes the seat of a man who leaves.
She touches the screen of a video game,
winning and losing. Another man watches her
or the game, it's hard to tell.
His Hofbrau sits still. A tram halts outside in its box of light.
Paul McCartney sings another scorn-worthy song
about a long and winding road, take me to your door.

NICARAGUA

The pudgy faced young man is at my Toronto door
He holds a small vase of roses. Thickly Québécois,
he says he's selling roses to raise money
so he can go to Nicaragua as an aid worker in the fall.
The roses are two dollars each.
He lives at 23 up the street and often at night,
sometimes by day, I see him walking up and down,
hands in pockets, straw-hatted sometimes,
sometimes not. Or on a bike, pack on his back.
From the distance of my doorstep it's impossible to tell
if it's Nicaragua
                he's going to or coming from.

HOW ARE THINGS ON BOUVET ISLAND?

And how are things on Bouvet Island?
Do the waves wash per usual?
Do rocks halloo to penguins?
Did Bouvet de Lozier decline to land,
aware it was just too far?
Did George Norris quickly reboard his ship,
a ship for anywhere?
What does Norway want with
landfall so useless in peace or war?
To live on Bouvet Island would be terrifying.
Is that why no one lives there?
Is it a place never here but always there?
Is it a place?

The remotest island in the world is Bouvet Island (Bouvetøya), discovered in the South Atlantic by J.B.C. Bouvet de Lozier on 1 January 1789, and first landed on by Capt. George Norris on 16 December 1825. Its position is 54°26's, 3°24'E. This uninhabited Norwegian dependency is about 1,050 miles from the nearest land – the uninhabited Queen Maud Land coast of eastern Antarctica. *Guinness Book of Records*

LOOP IN THE RIVER

A hutment by the river,
a pot stirring, and smoke.
The boats go by, an idle gaze
from the sliding deck
but no one watches from the shore.
So long a snare, it's a slip-knot now.
The huts will be gathered in,
people squeezed out
if they should prove of use.

LIGHTS OF CASTRIES

Every few years a hurricane abolishes history
and it all starts again, the lights
of the watery prism, glints of the barracoon.
On the hillside, from the dense green
made denser in darkness, come threep, threep
toc toc of ongoing animals. Somewhere
someone's weaving a mat, carving a coconut
the same as always, and someone else is promised
a delivery, an object, a service soon from now
meaning next hour, next day, or never.
People learn to be patient, or be a patient.
Everyone's hypochondriacal, ills often
just the climate (there is no weather) dusty sun
a radiant wall, shelter that menaces,
and pregnancies are like nine-month annunciations.
Night and day snap on and off, soon
dawn, a window blind rattling to the top
and then the sun's fierce grin zipped
by the equator, zapping the epidermis. Purdah
fires burn on the midden
common on which drift gross pig, stunted sheep.

Vans beep, gun for streetwise chickens,
always miss them. Those birds have the most road sense
on the island except the cocks in Sunday cockfights
who've got no sense at all. Down the road drivers
bathe their cars in bilharzia streams.
Mothers flock at streetcorner pumps as
children slant to school past
garbage gutters, yard rubble, diesel nimbus
and how do little girls, all starched blouses

crisp-pleated skirts, bleached socks, shine
this clean? At night
lights are flung to other islands along
a chain, necklace, diadem, of diamond, pearl,
sequin, rhinestone. On the south peak
the lighthouse on Moule-à-Chique
sweeps the channel to St. Vincent. Light Caribbean
mates dark Atlantic, and here in Castries
the so-called north, lights on the bridge
of yachts may be a bridge to Martinique, like
the Africançais people speak, patois
kitchen markets. Cars pause abreast
on mineshaft roads, chat like pastured horses.
Groggy from last night's rumshop, they crack open
a green coconut, drink the milk
whatever they drink at the pink Club Med stockade
scuba disco where the packaged grill on
grated volcano sand. That's one crop
for the once slave sugar island shaped
like an avocado, the other
indentured bananas, green figs going nowhere.
Harbour riding lights,
airstrip running lights,
cargo cult for those who while by dock and terminal.
Ever always earth and sea: pot fish
ground provisions, seasoning peppers. Talk
round the table, in the bush, cool off
wait, walk slow, tomorrow
shrivelling sun or pounding rain, no wind
and then the big one.

St. Lucia

THE ARRIVAL

At the airport the arrival is a scene in relief.
The new man strides to the foreground,
grasps his swirling tie, his dark suit rumpled,
long dark hair swept back, streaked natural white
above quizzical brow cued for action,
tan laced boots proof against the desert grit.
He looks one way. The man he supplants
looks another, hands in pocket,
the small buzz saw body of the retired general,
chewing over the past three weeks,
pen in his shirt pocket. His glasses are rectangular,
he moves on tiny feet.
                    Always there is background.
At the new man's shoulder plods in cap and shades
a rhomboid figure, relaxed finger on
a ventilated skeletal machine, barrel slanted –
not enough hands for the holstered gun.
He smiles, like the tall gent behind
in floppy hat and shoulder bag, perhaps a PR man
affable, bemused, and casual, here on another gig.
Others stare severally, mouths pursed, eyes obscured.
A token woman's largely concealed.
Their pant legs belled, their shoes thick-soled,
their laces intricate, they are here in one body.
They are walking into sand and wind.

TELEVISION

The camera shows us a procession to the grave,
the mourners in casual clothes, feet
in a woven shuffle, mouths in a complex song,
the shouldered coffin swaying.

The slain young man was a leader. Among
his friends and followers is a boy
who rightly or wrongly they blame for the killing.

The mourners, all young and handsome,
follow him back to his home.
He goes inside. The rest, their voices a storm,
surround it. One has a stick and with
a long sweep, careless, controlled, takes out the window.
The glass falls like rain, you can see the tinkle.

Then, suddenly, he's outside and the rest
surround him, and their pokes, shoves, cuffs
seem almost playful, his face almost but not quite terrified,
but then the camera picks up in someone's hand
a knife, the others closing in.

This act of revenge they will bear away
on thin shoulders like a coffin
once the closed circle opens and the lens moves off,
in their midst the crumpled boy.

GOOD FRIDAY

2 April 1999

It is Good Friday, though maybe not so good
because Serbs are bad.
We're bombing them. We are doing good.

Since few doubt that Nazis were bad
we will compare Serbs to them.
Such comparisons are good.

Our bombing will help the Albanians,
who are good, whereas Serbs are bad and getting badder.
Yet despite precise and powerful good bombs
the Serbs insist on staying bad.

To assist Albanians we bomb their capital.
As humanist good humanitarians
we aid them as much as our budget permits
once they become good refugees.

The bridge over the Danube at Novi Sad
is a long way from Kosovo
but because bridge and river
are used by bad Serbs
we have destroyed it, which is good.

Through its long history Belgrade
was often turned to rubble,
which was sometimes good and sometimes bad.
When our missiles hit it now it's good.

Bad Serbs have seized three good soldiers
and intend to put them on trial.
This looks bad, even for the Serbs.

In Kosovo the situation is bad and getting worse.
Soon we may have to order our men
to die on bad ground
to prove how good we are.

SERBIAN HEADSTONES

In limestone, marble, sandstone
they emerge in unrelieved relief:

carved achondroplastic dwarf pecked by doves
midget with belted knives and guns
soldier with rifle and sabre
carpenter with adze
teacher with an open book
woman with distaff
carter with whip

What they were is.
What they are was
wealth, class, work.
They live here swarmed by stone.

THE MAN ON A HORSE

Get out of the way, it's the man on a horse,
bulked with muscle, feet welded to stirrups.
He is flexed armour, his right arm stretched toward
what his army's just won on the battlefield.
He receives the keys to the fortress
and must be careful not to drop them.
He leads his troops, other men on horses,
in the van of men on foot or, tall against the sky,
perhaps he tells them all to turn around.
The horse is also larger than life, snorting,
one hoof lifted, fetlocks like wings.
The man and the horse have paused in triumph,
long enough to be cast in bronze.
The man on a horse crowns the square.
At his feet a dog sleeps,
refusing to wake up.

TWO SERBIAN GIRLS AT THE SALONIKA CEMETERY

You stand, looking solemn at the gates,
slimly monumental.
What's your loveliness doing here?
You did not fill these graves.
To pose for a photo is one thing.
To be an emblem for a nation is another.
That nation took a life at Sarajevo,
gave its life for France, and you are meant
to plight its memory. You are made to
be everything that nation is. You'd rather
turn your mind to music, jobs, and boys.
The nation will not let you. New wars
will make the past your future.
Inside, each headstone bears
an etched figure of one fallen.
Outside, your slim shoulders will carry it
as you give your sons to die young
while you go on, your
daughters at the cemetery gates
tomorrow, as beautiful as you.

TAXI RIDE

Saturday night the cab driver was chatty and cordial to the two visiting Englishwomen of late middle age. He spoke knowledgeably of Princess Diana and other members of the royal family. He felt sorry for Princess Di: her much older and experienced husband should have had more patience. He'd been watching a documentary on Queen Elizabeth, he was impressed how beautiful she was when young; it was her black hair, she wouldn't have been nearly so beautiful had she been blonde. Was England hilly or flat? He'd lived in many countries, but he'd never been to England, he'd wanted to go to school there but it cost too much, which is why he'd come to Canada. Driving past a park he warned the ladies not to take a short cut through it when they returned to their hostel that night. Not that they'd be harmed, but they might see things they wouldn't want to. When they got out, he bid them say hello to England for him when they returned, since he and his people had a special historical connection with it. He was Palestinian.

PALESTINIANS

What they are, not where they are
is who they are. Who
they are is a target
and they are running.

What they had
was taken away
and where they are
they will not have, ever.

Who they are is not hallowed
by a holy book, and those who believe
in the book they do have
often are their enemies.

Wherever they sleep, walk,
eat is trouble. The drone of planes,
the siege of a camp, a falling bomb,
a stone from a slingshot

repeats their name.
It is enough that Palestinians
are there, that they say
who they are.

GENOCIDE

They did not always paint memorably, or play concerti
on patiently restored instruments of the 18th century,
nor did they write acceptably universal humanistic novels
or devote themselves to scientific research for mankind's benefit.
Some of them, let us admit, would normally be locked away,
certified deranged, retarded, or merely criminal.
Some were inclined to cheat you on the purchase of a bedroom
    suite,
in a railway station your pockets would not be safe from them.
Standards of personal hygiene often fell short.
Some had warts, pimples, unpleasing body odours,
carried and spread the less condonable social diseases,
slobbered, gawked, picked their noses and sampled the harvest.
Some were not particularly articulate – loud, gauche, ignorant,
or bigoted. Some were simply boring.
 Or, if we look at other continents, may we assume
they always lived exemplary tribal lives of natural simplicity,
or tolerated those who threatened traditional hunting grounds.
They failed to observe standards of civilized warfare we expect.
In some districts, torture or slavery were not unknown.
On occasion, they abandoned elders or exposed unwanted young.
Every now and then they ate their prisoners.
They distended upper lips with plugs, sliced off labia.
There were, in fact, many ways in which they earned our
    disapproval,
just as far away in cities, others get conspicuously bad grades
from you or I or whoever scores the tests.
Like the beautiful, the kind, the talented, they too were butchered.

FORMS OF LOSS

Begin with a button off your best shirt.
Or: your mate, car, children
born and unborn. Someone steals your luggage,
a kind of rape. The first time is the worst.
Then later it seems you're better off without
freedom, but then freedom is illusion
so we're back with what we started
to love, honour, and cherish,
the end that void which turns questions into answers.
Some day we will find ourselves there
someone else's lost enquiry.

Is there anything more than leaving and losing,
parting and packing,
framing the last photograph?
When we came it was to move and remove,
so also when we went.
Where the picture hung
is now a nail in the plaster.
That, too, is a picture.

Loss is given us, and we take it.

IF HE GOES BACK

If he goes back it must be with some diminishment.
What had been part of him has shrunk, the houses lower,
the people fewer, brought down by chance or punishment.
He now knows these people so habitually rise and fall
it's hard to sort out the living from the slain.
He'd like to rise with them, but doesn't know
how high they will aspire, or if the skies will rain
upon them in some unforeseen and unsuspected hour
like the one he lived through once before.
He sees they're like people who stubbornly disdain
to leave a hurricane coast, tornado belt, or flood plain
because outside a blackened cellar or a shattered wall
is something they call home. And is that all?
He cannot tell, nor tell what he may owe
to memory and tomorrow, what is brought or sent
and whether when he goes and comes he's walking tall.

THE HISTORY OF MODERN EUROPEAN POETRY

I am heartily tired of them, these European poets,
their quest for absolutes, their pure intentioned
lines packed with content ethical, aesthetic,
symbolic, metaphysical. Though elsewhere others suffer
nowhere such refinement of suffering,
degradation, indigence. Syphilis, dope, dipsomania
the emblems of medieval guilds. I weary
of warfront suicides, gulags, internment camps,
entire countries down the toilet of isms and ologies.
The catastrophic loves, the early incest, the
last this, the final that, language inclusive and exclusive,
how silence is statement, how
impurity is programmatic. Dismayed
by such intelligence, stamina, and diary-keeping,
tuberculosis, orphanhood.
How much better had they been in America
where with virile voices we
yodel ditties in the slipstream of our own wind.

AT THE SITE OF AN AIR DISASTER MEMORIAL

Ahakista, Ireland, 23 June 1998

They hunch in the slashing rain
as they have on this date for 13 years
of wind and sun and rain.
The plane fell the time it is now. 8:13.
Passengers dropped into puddled pity, a pool of grief.
Helicopters winched them up,
families who ended their holiday,
women with babies born and unborn,
worried hopeful brides and grooms
now wedded to water. On wings
they went to Cork City where,
like clouds today, they lay in shrouds.
But aluminum shards littered the choppy sea.
Umbrellas roof the bereaved, each sheltering slope
a waterfall. The tiny hearts of fuchsia hedges bleed
and the pilgrims weep for the unredoable,
the crazy sorrow of death sentences.
The men who checked bags that blew the plane apart
coiled like a turban in the narrow windings
of conspiracy. Treading in tiny circles, they live in a public cell.
One was shot dead, a stupid kind of justice.
Behind bars another's learned to make pizza, a useful skill.

In the dispersed village with the Sanskrit-sounding name
the Om rises and fills the Irish monsoon.
Last night in Bantry, switchback curves away, mourners
met the Town Commissioner who gave bronze castings of
    cottagers
to the Canadian Ambassador down from Dublin,

the tall natty Indian chargé d'affaires,
and flowers for their wives. Are carnations and roses
reused for wreaths heaped on the sundial? Do
castings weigh down the dead beneath the waves?
Film crews hurtle the Forgotten Peninsula,
film pilgrims at a lighthouse on the rocky southwest tip
or the soft routines of choosing at the florist's.
Sound mikes and shouldered cameras hover
near self-catered curry-making. Maybe the recipe will be
cattle and seascapes, samosas and soda bread, or else indict
spastic forensic dozing. We will see.
The rain falls like rivets. County dignitaries
say they share the pain, priests intone prayers.
Those who lost are strangely bonded
in accusation and lament.
The rain may be rain, it may be tears.
At last a choir of sodden mites sings a Gaelic hymn.
The wading through mud to bogged cars,
we drive to a community hall and kindly sandwiches.
Next day sun, broken cloud, a breeze
flapping flags, palms, and pines.
Among the wreaths tiny plastic squares clutch photographs.
The petals and pictures are flying to India.

PLACES BY THE ROAD

> "*the material of experience is not the material of expression*"
> – Samuel Beckett

Up in the high woods,
past one more bend,
is a place by the road.
Under tall trees it fronts the road
and backs onto a green ravine.
Smoke curls from a shack
in which a sheep slowly spins.
A waterwheel moistens the meat
that people eat in booths mere steps away.
Those who pause use the washrooms,
and watch logging trucks toil up the grade.
Buses load or unload ladies
in kerchiefs and ankle-length dresses.
The cards on the buses say Srbrenica.
To write about such places is to make romances.
It is not so romantic to live in one.

PART III

HERE

Lord, it is good for us to be here...
— MATTHEW 17:4

WELCOME TO CANADA

□□□□□□□□□□□□□□□□

□□□□□□□ □□ □□□□□□

□□□□□□□ □□ □⇒□⇒□⇒

=⌐⌐╫╫╟╙ ╷╫ ╓┘╩╖┘

⌐┘┌ ┌┐ ╫╫╫

□□⋯⌠⌠˙∵⋮□ □˙∵ ⌠⌠□∵˙⎺λ□

☦☜☹☝☞✸☀ ❄☂ ☝☠☢☮✌☝

▶☘♀🏠👂🌵 💼♪ 🏰🌊🏛🏯

✘✂✁✃✄ ✓✎ ✂✍✄✌⌛

ÌÆêÅÈËÆ îÈ ÅÀëÀåÀ

WELCOME TO ΧΑΝΑΔΑ

WELCOME TO CANADA

THEMES ON A VARIATION OF SNOW

Snow is the converse of the dark

•

Of itself, snow is tautological

•

The iron hush that comes before heavy snow

•

The first snowfall
feathers trees, enormous delicate birds
and flakes, the forms of mist
slant against the steeple.
Soon church bricks will be slots,
pigeonholes, as birds shake wet from wings.
The apartment cliff's blotting paper
absorbs its nestlings.
The grey falling sky's concealed light
churns white to fill the world with it.
Wind lifts a green, an orange, a scarlet leaf
mulching the dovecotes.
Traffic purrs, unravelling storm.
A mauve-turbaned man emerges from swirl.
He fills a tank with gasoline,
with the air full of flight.

•

The fat flakes twirl
or winnow up down across.
They may be demonstrating
chaos or catastrophe theory.
they may simply be themselves

or in some way
be trying to change the world.

•

SnO

Tin pannikins lost from the overturned canoe of a voyageur between 1801 and 1802 were recovered 4.5 m below the surface of the water at Boundary Falls, Winnipeg River. Some of the surfaces of the pannikins have a thin crust consisting of white crystals and black crystals. The black crystals give an x-ray powder pattern identical to that of SnO. The mineral, named romarchite, was previously unreported in nature.

•

And often we would go down to the big cold lake. The pavilion was closed, the lake-facing veranda a rink. During the war soldiers on leave would quit the dance floor, lean over the railing to smoke and gaze across dark water that seemed to stretch to Europe. They would launch their spent cigarettes in the air, briefly fireflies before hissing out, hardly heard above the wave-lap.

The waves are there, but in lateral movement, and the ice in slabs and slates tinkle, clink. We slide and slip on the glazed snow before reaching the shore's foothold of grimy sand. Then we lob crusts of bread into the air and the gulls, off-white, grey, piebald, hover just above our heads, grabbing in their gaping beaks white bread.

VICTORIA DAY

The distant gunfire of Victoria Day
rattles across our risible kingdom
once more to trumpets and alarums
though the enemy is conquered,
having not got out of the way.
Where are the pillbox hats in the West?
The bearded frock coats of the East?
Gone in smoke puffs of backyard fireworks,
Roman candles of a fizzled empire.
We are all alone in the world,
lost without our snipers,
where the action isn't, no loss perhaps.
Better the kids have blameless fun.
Once you've lit it stand back,
stay away from that burning wick.

MODEL

On its mile of track on a scale of ¹/₄₈
the Model Railroad Club of Toronto
is showing how the province or at least the country
or at least the world
should be run.

Beside their trains engineers sedately glide,
keeping time, and in his booth above
the dispatcher sets the clock.

From busy Lilleyburg,
railyard southern terminus,
steam or diesel trains
travel down the valley,
cross creeks and rivers loop and disappear
into a tunnel, scoot across
suspension bridge
northbound
to Ebertville.

Main line to branch line,
mine to feed mill,
sawmill to dock,
a lake freighter rides an unruffled surface,
tourists inspect a quarry,
old cannery new restaurant.
All is industry,
never idle ever productive
and though the Central Ontario Railway
is near perfection much
remains to be done.

In this former munitions plant
modellers do piecework:
tracks and sidings, a steel deck bridge,
more switches and scenery,
new paint factory, coal trestle, another paper mill.

An unseen hand carves the rock face,
lays the bed.
There is rest in such activity.
The world would be a better place if
the Model Railroad Club of Toronto were running it.
Any train is walking distance
and a trip takes 15 fifteen minutes.

CHINATOWN

The cheerful stinks,
the windows' barbecued zoo,
the there brought here.
The city is a vast stomach
and Chinatown is its waistline
and Chinatown is for eating
and eating is good.

TORONTO

The streets are nice. They're safe.
There are lots of things to do.
You can jog, play softball,
listen to jazz and for a time
it'll take your mind off the city.
A city this good can't be all bad.
You may get a chance to enact fantasies.
He will provide the garter belt.
She, the dog collar and leash.
After, you can go to a restaurant.
You'll pay for the matches, pay for the mints,
soon you will be décor yourself
and people will pay for you.
There are municipal by-laws
against smoking, staring, washing car windows.
Can't the rest of the country wake up and
just call itself Toronto?
Some people in Manhattan speak
of a new concept in Toronto,
something that worked there.
Don't think we can't teach them a thing or two.
The CN Tower, world's highest self-supporting structure,
winks like a god at night.
Only scared people build this tall.

FROM AN AUCTION CATALOGUE

Here is some furniture for our lives.
These are continents gifted from anonymous makers.
We have made for them a thing called a market.
They will buy what they have sold.
One day they'll like us and be like us
householders of the painted, gilded, carved,
parquetry and marquetry.
We are buying and selling what was brought to us.
The listed objects are our own
to dine, dress, write, walk, wash, and sleep
over and on, our tinted sepulchres of taste,
chairs and tables our fashion and our permanence.
In the corner cabinet stand our skeletons,
a "Pair of Venetian-style Painted Bronze Blackamoors."

KOSOVO

The roof-inspecting raccoons,
the scuttling mice in rivet-holes of subway rails,
the fox with a duck in her mouth trotting under
the thundering overpass
(lucky day for the fox, unlucky for the duck)
these are proof of something.
Maybe joy, maybe coexistence.
We dwell within loud mumbling machines
but there's all this life around us.
None of it asks us for names,
or when to go and when to stay.
They have means to their ends,
their ends are sufficient.
The cat rakes its caws on the backyard lumber,
stretching its length on the length of the plank
and what's it to you? The cat
would say if a cat could say.
These animals teach lessons of the adequate
but the great thing is they need not preach.
Perhaps I make too much of this,
though it's irresistible
to interject the personal
to draw a moral,
sum it up,
and speak for that which lives among us,
those we happen not to be.

HAMMOCK

In a small damp cave a Mayan maiden
is weaving a hammock just for you.
From large sharp spines she finds a shape,
with care she pleats the sisal.
The decisions of her fingers serve
your transit to and fro and back and forth.
Inside moist dimness her round brown hands
guard against your accidents,
how a pair of you could, like dogs,
become conjoined end to end,
not knowing how you got into this fix
or how to get out of it. She knows a hammock
can catch you up like a fishing net,
or turn you into a whirling spindle.
The Mayan maiden herself sits in a hammock.
She bends as it sways. The hammock she makes,
anchored to trees, will be a sieve for air
and keep you halfway to heaven.
You must trust to her hands, that what she does
will bear and move the weight that's you.

IN THE PROVINCES

The chapped lives of small-town girls
shed successive skins of purity
What do you expect?
That's how it's done in the provinces.

The teeth of the neighbour's kid
could peck corn through a screen door
but just the same there are some awful pretty girls
driving trucks in the provinces.

In places called the Coffee Pot
the boys order a hot waitress to go
and lives reach out in an endless ellipse.

The watched girls thread by on spindles.
Do their nights flare with the cupped flame
of a man simply pausing, lighting up? Or does
it all end on a road in ruts back of the golf course?

Farmers regularly drive their cars down embankments.
It's a way of making sure of a new car every year
and how they tell if you're any good in the provinces.

The big cities look down on the little cities.
The little cities look down on the towns.
The towns look down on the country
and some people in the big cities
want to move to the country
because they think there's something good in the provinces.

The old folks aren't after a fast buck,
they look for moral triumphs
are obsessed with weather and funerals,
or dispossessed.

The kids commute two hours a day
to modular blocks that get bigger and smaller,
wave good-bye to the old folks' motel
bigger and smaller, awaiting some news.

Some parts want to split away
and some parts want to stay
but it's all the same in the provinces.

The seas are slick with oil
from TV production crews
who film each other drilling,
the rancid pulp mills
poison the veins of earth
for mines go deep in the provinces
and all the commercials are made there.

As a public relations move the pulp companies
hacked out cross-country ski trails
but one of these days they'll spray skiers
confusing them with the spruce budworm
then they'll have to reschedule re-schedule
because the Book of Ecclesiastes was written in the provinces
though a time to die is everywhere.

The player-piano winds say not much here
but the disco-bomp of bouncing snowmobiles
that search for fine days, deep snow, and shell ice.

Rabbit snares offer a grammar of these woods,
the blood lust of indifference
The curb-kissed city kid, the man hunting coons in the corn
are brother provincials, hooked on death,
smear on the snare.

You think the whales are in troubles?
The elephant poachers are spiking bananas.
with battery acid,
clearing the earth of the damned things.
We need more paved roads in the provinces.

I will try to learn the language of the provinces.
I speak it imperfectly.
No one's ever plumbed the subtle desolation
of a road crew's back road half-built house,
nor has anyone ever scaled
the cruddiness of ziggurats.

WHITEFACES: 1982

At every sight the blank tinnitus,
chromatic ennui of whitefaces.
Walking downtown, one sometimes sees
black or yellow or red, but
in town the whiteface librarians stamp books,
white merchants sell skim-milk merchandise.
If I, a white face, am bored,
think of the depthless boredom a blackface
feels enveloped by white.

To pick up a black hitchhiker.
can bring dark odours inside a car.
One thing can lead to another:
a blackface coming home to supper
asking for a second helping, a blackface
dating your whey-faced daughter,
a blackface taking your job,
raping your wife, crapping in your garden,
borrowing sugar, dunning you for rent,
boll weevils in the oatmeal, famine
and pestilence, the common cold.

Whitefaces boring as Charolais or chalk pits.
I come from a long bleached line of Scots
Calvinists before Calvin.
Think of South Africa: black, coloured, colourless.
Or think of this village: whitefaces
buying groceries, whitefaces walking,
breathing heavily through whitemasks,
my neighbour, the Hereford steer across the road.

The vanilla people,
they grudgingly buy chocolate.
Only on television does a blackface appear,
and then as a visitor from another planet,
the Third World. After watching him,
the whitecouple repairs to whitesheets
for a ghastly copulation.
How can they sleep in the dark?
They add bleach to their wash.
They are 99 $^{44}/_{100}$ per cent pure.
The weather report says snow tomorrow.

HISTORY

Their Labrador pup strayed down a field
and got killed by a car.
My mother saw crows circle.
"I know what that means," she said.
She grieved for weeks.
My father grieved as well
but more briefly and explosively.
"I wouldn't care if they took out every
damn Mackenzie in the country
and shot him."
There you have it:
the close reading of animal signs,
private sorrow become tribal rage,
the history of Scotland.

NEW PLACE

The first night in the new place
my mother and I shared a bed
in the bare and jumbled parlour.
My father remained behind to do the final milking,
having sold the farm.
                          The minister's wife
kindly donated a pail of chicken soup
that, whether unskimmed or oversalted,
was deemed acceptable but unusable.
That first night was difficult.
Of course the tension of sleeping with my mother,
but also the pail
set in the corner, an offering for
the collie, uneasy himself
at coping with displaced terrain.
All night he padded a clear path
among the clutter, lapping at the pail,
unable to resist, incapable of stopping himself.
Slumped, he'd try to sleep
then return wearily, no rest but soup,
flap flap.

MR. SACHS

My uncle, the one who never harmed anyone
except himself, the one whom a postal employee
informed me was "the town drunk," too
extravagant a title for this one-eyed quiet man,
the one whose wife, on coming home, found he'd put
a pan of chops to bake for our supper, and dumped them
on the lawn to the surprise but pleasure of their dog,
the uncle who Gestetnered high school cribs and called
it "Maritime Extension College," which might have succeeded
    had not
a partner cheated him, had he not a taste for failure, this dead
    uncle
Mr. Sachs always cited when he cut my hair.
Adolph was Mr. Sach's first name, unpleasant reminder
of another European, whom he in no way resembled.
He was Czech, small, sleek, and dark, like a polite nutria,
his tidy shop annexed to his neat fine-boned wife's
beauty parlour. When Mr. Sachs fetched up in this straitened
    stony town
my uncle took the trouble to teach him English.
Mr. Sachs might have been impressed that
someone took an interest in an emigrant.
At any rate, he was ever grateful.
My uncle, who so often expressed himself in negatives –
who did *not* leave his wife to chill out in their big hilltop house,
who did *not*, as he might have done, club her to death,
for once had stressed the positive.

COLD HOUSE

Big cold house with a buffalo chair,
horns bound with rawhide straps like a torture instrument.
But torture would be something animate
a scream in childbirth, fecund.
Here lived my pompous kindly uncle
with his frigid horror of a wife.
The verdigris false teeth of my relative by marriage
juts like a sore on her savage lips.
Why did they marry?
Were they the only college graduates around
and hence forced to mate?
Suspecting pregnancy, she said "If I am he'll pay for it."
She wasn't, but he paid anyway.
A gentle sarcastic man resigned to one blind eye,
his dingy little town,
a stroke made him silly.
He died and didn't leave a will.
He never had one.
Sloppy lord of the beer rings
on Canadian Legion tables
he had his triumph there,
to pronounce correctly,
to ask for "a good cigarette."
In their courting days they exchanged love letters.
For a Legion banquet he put a rose in his lapel.
She snarled, "Not appropriate."
Perhaps it wasn't.

CLASSMATES

Among Mackenzies, Macleans, and Macdonalds
was a Mogensen, a Lindblad, and a Mansour.
Mogensen was a Dane, eyes blue and bloodshot,
famed for boozing through our high school nights.
Lindblad was a Swede, a tall bully,
jeering, fearsome, yet almost likeable.
Mansour was a handsome Lebanese,
trouble-prone, much picked on by Mrs. Elliot,
she the slasher of chalky algebra along the board.
When they graduated, what became of them?
Well, Mogensen disappeared.
Lindblad led a fishermen's union.
Mansour's sister married a crown prince of Jordan.

HEATHBELL SCHOOL REUNION

We have gathered for something valuable
in Nova Scotia
though what this might be is hard to say.
The work's to whack the dust off as we once did
the blackboard brush, motes spinning,
to sprinkle Dust-Bane, faintly moist, across the floor
and sweep, and sweep, and sweep.

Today we commemorate a schoolhouse.
How could one small room have held us all?
We who grew beneath its roof
retrieve chronology,
the date of the stoked stove's installation,
the date the two-hole outhouse
doubling as a coal shed became operative.
Both were painted white.
We were among the last to go to such a school.

For some hours I plausibly belong
to a tribe unwilling to shock one another,
on a day of warm half-truths.
Toward the end of our nostalgic afternoon
I'm singled out, stand to reminisce
about the outhouse, in which I spent much time confined.
I forget to add that my son's teacher doesn't
each morning dole out cod-liver oil
or stick a gold-star on a ruled line
if fingernails were clean.
Everyone looks much younger now
than they ought to. We're all the same age.

Part of the entertainment's a skit
as in the Christmas concerts we used to stage.
The curtain rattles across the wire (we strung a blanket).
A diner in a flowered hat complains to an aproned waitress
about the hairs she's found in the oxtail soup.
Waitress: "Well, of course. What do you expect
if you drag an oxtail through water?"
Barnyard humour. Why not?
We came from barnyards.

For us a woman's hand-made a booklet
bound with a ribbon. She got the idea from my mother.
My mother loved occasions.
I keep wanting to debrief her, the evening drawing in.
A retired veterinarian talks about my parents.
A quiet man – it's astonishing to hear the flow,
how my father was always calm
no matter what, how they sacrificed
to care for my cerebral-palsied brother.
I take it in, a smile on my face.

Swaddled, from houses clinched by elms,
we waddled the dirt, mud, snow,
left behind horror, misery, and kindliness,
entrapment and contentment, the weather
and work. Then, later, the speeding bicycle.
One classmate, once with the mustiness of poverty,
is a solid poised lady now, and another,
who thumps the piano at old-time dances,
accuses me of having been the boy who put
libellous graffiti on the outhouse wall.
And here's the gangling bachelor, a buddy
who, the last time I lived here,

took a grudge against me, wouldn't say why.
Blank-faced, he ignores me,
and I see him go round the corner with a friend,
half-grinning, gawping, head bobbing.
eager for converse, or maybe a drink.
I make excuses for my absent eldest brother,
always better liked than me.
A video slides box camera snapshots past us
to the tune of "California Dreaming" –
California-dreaming, up to the ass in drifts.
We see dark glimpses of teachers
who wound among our anchored desks,
a grade at a time, the one who told me
I was too smart to be a farmer.

The long table's spread with cookies and crustless sandwiches
cold this warm bright day. On dusty shelves
cans of Campbell's had been ranged
for noon hot lunches. Ice cream's no longer
little tabbed tubs inside a big wadded case
that, when unclasped, released a dry-ice fogbank,
the treat at games that closed each year of school.
Potato-bag races, three-legged races, wheelbarrow races
across short grass.
We'll not meet again, that way at least.

What have we made of these beginnings?
We haven't found an answer
but at least we ask. Well, I shouldn't speak for others.
Yet it's in our scattering directions.
The school stands at the crossroads.
The latched door opens, and we go in.

DUNROBIN

Golspie, Sutherlandshire

Down among the steam pipes of Dunrobin Castle
we of the Clan Sutherland
gather to learn the melancholy facts of Highlands history.
We're fed jerky beef and potato salad
to songs, skits, and recitations.
There's a piper, of course,
who's given a glass of whisky
and appears to be grateful.

A speaker informs us that the rise of Protestantism
"spread superstition in the Highlands."
A baritone regales us with "The Nut Brown Maid"
and thank God a lady from Aberdeen's
brought a mickey of Ballantine's in her handbag.

At The Sutherland Arms,
surrounded by beak-nosed Sutherlands,
I breakfast on finnan haddie.
Later, the Dunrobin doorkeeper informs me
that the Highlands could never have supported its population.
They had to go.
The alternative was to send the bleeding sheep to Nova Scotia.

This moment his castle's populated
by Raeburn portraits and tiger skins.
The first part of the century
ducal Sutherlands took up destruction of big game.
The museum back of the castle

allows one to view the curious remains
of numerous now-extinct birds and animals.

Across the road one finds the statue
of the Second Duke of Sutherland, a railway buff
who built a track so he could drive the train
that brought his gracious Queen to see the sights,
her gillie, too.
In a hall slides of attractive crofts flash,
we're lectured by a fellow from the university.
He gets a present, as does
the Countess of Sutherland, a wraith in black
who seems nice enough and gracefully accepts a basket,
ostensibly containing fruit.

Above flower-garden stone-wall Golspie
one may observe, a Christ of the Andes among the clouds,
the monument to the First Duke of Sutherland
"erected by a grateful tenantry."
His factor, Patrick Sellar, who didn't have the Gaelic
sicked dogs on the less grateful.

Rotten tubs slowly hauled
the boat-huddled windblown to newfound rocks and roots
like Original Sin. The Clearances.
All clear for the landed who,
given chance, choice, money, and bright ideas,
find that people in the way

never are sleek as the Countess of Sutherland's Holsteins,
munching complacently on the savoury grass.

ODE TO THOMAS JEFFERSON SUTHERLAND

Those who didn't know him well
thought well of him.
Not so those who knew him well,
men like himself,
muddled and enthusiastic,
not so much indecisive
as making too many decisions,
sometimes all at once.

Through the fog of fervour
or opportunism, which,
it was hard to tell, but
in which he and his fellows
hid themselves,
he's glimpsed at
one of his many trials,
"dressed in a blue blanket coat
under which he wore
a Kentucky hunting shirt with
two tawdry epaulettes on his shoulders."

December 5th was central to his life.
On that day in 1821 he joined the
marines, in nine years rising
to the rank of sergeant.
In upstate New York he learned the printer's trade
but became a "lawyer of low standing."

On December 5th, 1837 York's
revolting farmers southward tramped
Yonge Street ruts with pikes and cudgels,

staves and pitchforks.
Fresh from a tavern putsch
the hothead redhead Mackenzie
led the snorting herd

armed with a perfect constitution.

The same day Sutherland spoke to raise
an "Independent Canadian Service" in Buffalo,
a change though not a rest from
trimming anti-Masonic sheets in the wind.
After all he'd fought with Simón Bolívar
or so he said, adding
"Shall we withhold our sympathies
and as individuals our assistance?"

No, but it ended badly.
The routed Mackenzie fled, his printing type
distributed across the lake.
In Buffalo, squabbles about recruiting
and stealing arms from city hall
and a river island occupied
from which orders were issued,
ignored or countermanded.
In Cleveland, Sutherland told a crowd
how the Queen's
bloodthirsty savages attacked
"our unoffending brethren adjacent to
the Canadian frontier."

His proclamation offered
300 acres, $100 in silver,

"all the blessings of freedom"
for his volunteers but
at Detroit the freedom fighters
saw their schooner grounded near
the fort they meant to capture.
Brig.-Gen. Sutherland declined
to rescue his fellow patriots
and staunchly ordered a retreat.

Everybody but Sutherland
blamed Sutherland.
His men voted him least likely to succeed.
He was collared for breaching neutrality.
In the dock, a reporter said,
"of large stature with dark hair and complexion
he was a very fine specimen of the genus homo."

Not guilty in that court he resigned
a non-existent command,
then was captured on the river ice.
Sure the British would shoot him,
he sliced veins in his hands and feet.
Useless bloodshed. The verdict was
transportation to Van Diemen's Land
with other Tasmanian devils.

But justice fogged around Sutherland.
Claiming he'd been misled,
he whined to the governor.
A fellow inmate said his "bad conduct and
attempts to quarrel with everyone
in the room, his lying, his vanity and

assumption of importance, as well as
his playing the spy upon us
made the men all despise him."

The trial had been bungled.
Ordered set free if he gave security he
wouldn't re-enter British soil,
he couldn't raise it.
To hell with it and him.
They let him out at Cornwall,
more trouble than he was worth.

Across the line, back in the rag trade,
he published gusty pamphlets, letters to and by the editor,
sheaves of poems, loose leaves.
Hunters' lodges tended the old musket flame.
Wrangles now over raising a regiment
to fight in California against Mexico,
somebody anyway.

For five years he vanished
then turned up in Midwest river towns,
a carpet-sack slung across his shoulders.
A figure out of Twain or Melville,
he churned the Mississippi,
paid his fare with phrenological lectures
for those who needed their heads examined.

Nebraska boomer,
in his head still swirled
life, liberty, the pursuit of happiness
though not for Indians,
who "had no right to keep such fine lands."

He proposed a "Military agricultural school"
to train revolutionists in Europe
and maybe grow grain.
Farther west he tramped, with him
a little girl named Viola, scooped up on his tour,
the ragamuffin pair shuffling dustily
into a mini-series.

At Iowa-and-Sac he died of typhus.
What was in his head had fled.
A trunk contained "a
large quantity of manuscript, made up of
biography, history
and poetry, much of it
seemingly prepared for the press."

The Savannah *Monitor* observed
he'd been "somewhat noted"
as "a fine scholar,"
"one of the leading spirits in the
Canadian rebellion."

Across the fitful screen I also write
the obit of my namesake,
a muddy figure lurching across the border,
time's corrected mistake.

ABOUT THE AUTHOR

Fraser Sutherland has made a practice of hanging around people who are as different as possible from him. Which may or may not be very surprising considering he is descended from an unbroken line of Highland Scots, was born in northern Nova Scotia, and has lived in Halifax, Ottawa, Montreal, and Nelson, BC. Of fourteen books, *Manual for Emigrants* is his eighth selection of poetry. His work has been translated into Albanian, Farsi, French, Italian, and Serbo-Croat. Fraser Sutherland lives in Toronto.

"Since I've long regarded myself as an internal exile, it was natural to interest myself in *real* exiles. It was also natural to find in immigrants the diverseness that has always held such appeal for me. It's unfashionable, even politically incorrect, to find 'the other' in foreigners or immigrants. To me, it's lifeblood. Otherness to me doesn't mean that the other is an exotic specimen to be dissected, exploited, or patronized. Connecting with the other is a way of connecting with the otherness within myself, a way of recognizing and validating difference. Ultimately of course we're all human beings."

– Fraser Sutherland, *Northern Poetry Review*, February 2007